PRAISE FOR BETSY L. JORDAN

"Being Betsy's client changed my outlook on life. There are self-help books, motivational movies, thoughtful quotes that give you a 'hmmm' moment, but there's nothing like the direct dynamic impact of Betsy's approach. There is such a thing as a mental shift, or altering your mind-set. I know this now, because Betsy Jordan helped me accomplish quite a shift with her unique coaching methods. Thank you Betsy for making all the difference in my world, I have a much better grasp on business and financial responsibility than ever before."

—Daniel Jones

"Betsy, brings a great energy and enthusiasm to her work. Creative, concise and fun to work with."

—Joseph C. D'Alessandro
Independent Media Production Professional

"I hired Betsy for executive coaching, and it was one of the best decisions I've made in a while. She revitalized key aspects of my career with her thoughtful and disciplined methodology. She is so intelligent and empathetic, yet she'll tell you when your full of sh*t when you need to hear it. I highly recommend her to turbo-charge your life."

—Chip Venters
CEO at BrowsePlay Interactive Video

"Betsy is an inspired leader with energy and passion to share her many gifts and talents. I recommend her without reservation."

—Denise Cline
Member at Law Offices of Denise Smith Cline, PLLC

"Betsy exemplifies the word *transformation* for that is what she offers all of her clients. Coaching with Betsy offers direct feedback and direct results!"

—Laura Gould
Owner/Coach at SwimLessonsRaleigh.com

"On a personal level, Betsy practices what she preaches. She never stops growing and learning."

—Will

"North Carolina's film industry was well served through Betsy's insight, hard work and commitment. Betsy championed projects that promoted the industry and was able to focus on the key issues that made a difference in how North Carolina competed against other states. She's a great ally to have on your team."

—Monty Hagler
President & CEO, RLF Communications

"Betsy Jordan is a visionary who can see beyond the routine tasks of the day. She has a gift for marketing and putting together resources to accomplish her goals. Betsy is a leader and can influence others with her keen insight, clear communication style and engaging personality."

—Bob Jamieson
Living Seaside Realty Group

"I was well served through Betsy's insight, hard work and commitment. She's a great ally to have on your team."

—Monty Hagler

"Betsy is a results oriented person, one you will be glad to have had the pleasure to meet, and delighted she's always working in your best interests."

—Carol Spiller, CMB

"Betsy Jordan has a keen insight into helping people achieve their life goals. She has an uncanny knack for breaking down barriers that may be creating obstacles for people that they cannot see for themselves: a frequent life-staller; spending time with Betsy is like drinking from a cold fountain on an incredibly hot day; you always want to come back for more! Take making a change in your life seriously and give Betsy a call; you won't be sorry!"

—Anna Watson Blair
Infusion Therapy Nurse at UNC-Hospitals

"Betsy is bright and highly intuitive. Her assistance with me at a critical point in my life's journey was instrumental in helping me in many areas, both professional and personal. Anyone hiring her will be rewarded many times over."

—Joe Christian
Performance Coach

"Betsy is an amazing business woman with dead-on intuition and a plethora of skills and experiences to draw from. I recommend her without reservation."

—Trish Thomas
CEO at Atomic20

"Betsy is a seasoned professional who brings her high energy level and professionalism to everything she does. Having her work with you and your company is a great investment."

—Teena Anderson
Non-Profit Organization Management Professional

KEY 6

PERSONAL POWER

WITH

COMPANION JOURNAL

BOOKS BY BETSY L. JORDAN

Seven Absolute Keys to Create Anything:!

Coach! Seven Keys for the Beginning Coach

Key 1, Oneness, with Companion Journal

Key 2, Inter-Dimension, with Companion Journal

Key 3, Movement, with Companion Journal

Key 4, Paradox, with Companion Journal

Key 5, Exchange, with Companion Journal

Key 6, Personal Power, with Companion Journal

Key 7, Yin/Yang, with Companion Journal

BullsEye!

The Seven Tactics To Hit The Bull's Eye In Your Business

Film Industry Professional's Edition

Book One: Connect!

Book Two: See!

Book Three: Act!

Book Four: Experience!

Book Five: Expand!

Book Six: Power Up!

Book Seven: Launch!

KEY 6

PERSONAL POWER

WITH

COMPANION JOURNAL

BY BETSY L. JORDAN

Dedicated to my remarkable *mentors*.
They had their work cut out for them!

"The man who trims himself to suit everybody will soon whittle himself away."

—Charles Schwab

CONTENTS

Author's Note...iv

PERSONAL POWER, THE SIXTH KEY........................1

Introduction 3

Personal Power..11

Lighthouse..17

Heroes..21

Boot Camp...25

Tread Softly..29

Conclusion 31

The 7 Keys 41

COMPANION JOURNAL...43

   Exercise ~ Be Your Superhero 47

   Exercise ~ What Stopped You?..............................57

   Exercise ~ Unlocking with The Keys 69

About Betsy Jordan..77

Start Today! 79

Seminars & Webinars 81

Coaching... 83

Acknowledgements... 85

The Chakras 89

The 7 Keys 91

7 Keys Summaries.. 93

    Key 1, Oneness... 93

    Key 2, Inter-Dimension.................................. 93

    Key 3, Movement 94

    Key 4, Paradox.. 94

    Key 5, Exchange 95

    Key 6, Personal Power.................................... 95

    Key 7, Yin/Yang.. 96

7 Keys & The Chakras 97

Success Stories.. 99

AUTHOR'S NOTE

Many coaches will understand the principles covered herein automatically. My desire is that coaches use these universal principles of creativity and develop a language to use in their practices, troubleshooting as they go along. For example, the client who understands "oneness" and networks easily, may need work in the area of "personal power" if they are networking for approval. Or, a client who has no trouble imagining their future (inter-dimension) who yet won't get up off of the sofa needs work in the area of "movement." Let the seven keys be your framework.

Betsy Jordan

PERSONAL POWER, THE SIXTH KEY

"He who controls others may be powerful, but he who has mastered himself is mightier still."

—Lao-Tzu

INTRODUCTION

The Difference

How many relationships, jobs, classes, experiences, great ideas, and coaching clients—even, have you experienced in your life? If we are alike in any way, you and I, it's probably safe to assume that we have both had great experiences and achievements, and have both had our share of failures and mishaps, too. In fact there is a lot that ten different jobs, three different careers, moving around the United States, one child, two stepsons, and two marriages will teach you, but the real difference came when I made a few simple changes in my life:

Focus and application.

As a positive, interested human being, I read, watched, listened, attended, and really did absorb a great deal of good information. Still, failure and success seemed somehow determined unconsciously and haphazardly until I focused on

3

what were emerging as key principals and made very sure I applied what seemed true enough to possibly be universal. *Keys* started to rise to the top of my experiences when I employed attentive focus with application. Thrilling—simply thrilling. And today I get to share what I have learned with you, because my life after that point of discovery has been different, to say the least.

Seven *keys* unlock those doors you might have fought to get to, only to find them locked—the few keys that open to your own treasure trove of manifested dreams. These are the few really important doors in life, doors that lead to your own creativity and ability. What others call "luck" is explained in these pages.

But you've heard that before, right? In fact the bookstores are full of books making that very same claim, so what's the difference? Why read this book and others in my series? Simple. *You.* Let's be honest, there is a glut of information—good information—out there and probably even in your own library or on your own Kindle, so why read more? Well, the fact that you *are* reading more tells me two things: for all the good advice you've already found you want more which means you likely have *still* not completely found the right answers for *you*, and second, I believe most advisors do not allow into their equations the most important variable, which is, as I've said, *you.*

I want you to take the Seven Keys and make them yours, to understand these Seven Keys and apply them in *your own* way and to your unique situations and relationships. I want you to find these keys so natural after a period of focus and application that they become second nature, and what others see as a "knack" or "luck" seem to follow you wherever you go. I want you to have your own Midas touch as a result of your new acquaintance with *the Seven Keys*.

And there are seven. Some say this is the number of the mystic and indeed, throughout the ages seven has had a special place in the world. God created the heavens and the Earth in seven days. The Greek God Hermes is credited with scribing an ancient text with seven natural laws. Life itself is often described as having a seven-year cycle (or a seven-year itch). And after all of my own research and observation, the number seven simply seems to present itself universally, and in profound and powerful ways. So, seven it is.

And I now know there is *power* and an ability to *consciously create* what I really want, what you really want. Things are different now, thanks to that *knowledge*. And it did transition from a *belief* to a *knowledge* after consistently getting results with the seven keys. And when I consider sharing this knowledge it strikes me that I have plenty in my own life I wish I had *not* created, but to shy away from these things, you'll see, only pulls us back into the trap that beleaguers

5

most people, the belief that we *cannot* create our own thoughts, that we cannot manifest our own beauty and even our own greatness. In fact, even today when I end up with something that I am not consciously creating, I know that I get to learn from it, but I also know I get to move on from there to consciously change my own thoughts in order to create something different, something desirable. I know that there is power and the ability to consciously create what I really want, when I am fully accountable for it all.

You choose: which is more empowering, when you blame circumstances or people around you for anything non-ideal in your life *or* knowing that you are responsible for all of your life *and can therefore change it?* Important choice to make. And your life is happening *now and you are in it*—this is not a "waiting room" by any means. Too many valuable people still see it that way.

In fact the former choice is actually the more practical one, and before you take any knowledge and consider it, it should, after all, be practical. All my roads have led me here. I have studied with various people, as mentioned I've read, listened, watched, attended, and I've experimented with my own life. I have things in my own background you would be very able to relate to: failures and successes. There are enough of the first that would make us empathetic friends, and plenty of the second that would establish my credibility to lead on this issue, to capture your imagination for self- and world-improvement, just as the discovery of these seven keys has captured mine.

Anyone can learn these seven keys, either for oneself or as a philosophy with which to help others. We all create our worlds subconsciously everyday anyway, why not take charge of that facility? This book is an attempt to give you the tools that I now apply in my own life and my own practice, and these tools can now be shortcuts for you and your own clients!

But it's not magic, either. Learning to be aware takes practice.

Although some very important parts of the process cannot be "seen," they are as real as those parts that you can see. In fact, the world of the "unseen" is arguably more important than the world of the "seen," and this will become more clear as we move forward. With each key that we explain you (and your clients) will be given a chance to work with it, to do exercises which give you a practical experience of the key. I have found—through my own experience and through information that frankly, has simply come through me—that each key has a corresponding chakra, or area in the energetic body to which it corresponds. The chakra system is an energetic system which is explained through Vedic science, and which the Hindu religion has located just outside of the body but close to very specific areas of connection. You can use these areas of the body as touch points to remember the Seven Keys. Other than that, please see the appendix on the chakras at the back of this book and visit texts on the chakra system to understand more about that connection. My intention here is to keep things simple.

The way that I believe creativity comes through most quickly is from the 7th chakra down. In other words, I believe creativity can best be explained from the spiritual plane through manifestation, from the intellectual to the material, and from head to toe. You have a thought, the thought becomes manifest after action is taken.

Yet you do not have to believe this to benefit from the exercises or the information. My intention is to give you the tools to build a foundation for creating the life you dream of, with confidence that you are in tune with the natural elements of the universe, and to do so as quickly as possible.

I wish you all you have ever dreamed of.

And once you've assembled your own *Seven Keys* with focus and application, how will your life be different? How will your coaching practice change? And who will you help?

"Tenderness and kindness are not signs of weakness and despair, but manifestations of strength and resolutions."

—Kahlil Gibra

PERSONAL POWER

Have you heard the phrase, "Don't give your power away," or "Hold on to your power?" Well I have a belief that serves me completely, and you don't have to adopt it if you don't want to, but I believe that you cannot give your power away. It's yours. You either use it or you don't. That's empowering to me because I can then at any moment go, "Whoa—how am I using my personal power right now? What am I using it for? Where is it I want to go and how is it that I can use my resources—my personal resources which includes energy, expression, voice, action and physicality?" I can choose how to use all of this at any time and I can shift from going, "Oh wow, let's see, are you using your personal power most effectively right now? Yes or no?" And if the answer is no, then shift. And I can shift like (snap!) that.

When we talk about personal power and we talk about it as if someone is taking something from us, remember, no one can control you—no one, ever. You always have the power of your thought. You always have the power of your energy and your expression, no matter what is happening to you. How you interpret things is important. Taking and separating fact from interpretation is critical.

I have conducted seminars and workshops based on this material, and in one of these workshops I had an attendee who had questions about a system, an institution that she was working in. And she had made up or interpreted some of the facts of the circumstances in a way that completely disempowered her. It was a completely disempowering way of thinking, but she did it to herself. It was not something somebody did to her, but her own thoughts, her own interpreting of these facts.

This institution had certain rules and certain policies and they were interpreted by the school system and could have been interpreted by some of the parents in a way that was not correct. She was also feeling like she was limited in terms of how she conducted her work so she felt like she had to do it within this system. And doing it within this system did not serve her ultimate vision for where she wanted to go with the creation of her work.

She needed to make a living and she needed to charge for her services, and within the school system this was frowned upon because you're using a public institution. She could probably have gone to a private school and do that and charge for her work. But what happened instead was she interpreted all of this as "They don't want me. They don't like me. My work's not good. I'm not a good person." All kinds of ways to interpret those facts that were not at all what the facts were. In fact it was very removed from the facts.

So in then going back and focusing on, "Okay, this is school policy. If I cannot do this here, how can I create my work in another fashion.?" she then saw that she was interpreting the facts the way she was and making up this belief about herself. Just the awareness of that made her realize, "Oh my gosh, I can open my business outside of this environment!" and other avenues opened up to her. You could see her physically rise up. She had completely disowned her own power, completely backed up and said, "Okay, this system is more powerful than me. These people's opinions are more powerful than me or my work!"

So when you are in question about where you are holding yourself in the world, creating every minute, or as someone who is holding themselves as a victim of circumstances, check in. What are the facts? How am I interpreting those facts? What beliefs am I making up about myself because of

13

the facts that I am interpreting this way? And once you do that, make a different choice, seek an interpretation of those facts that will take you forward in your life toward the vision that you have and toward the creativity that you really want to manifest in the world.

"It is better to conquer yourself than to win a thousand battles. Then the victory is yours. It cannot be taken from you, not by angels or by demons, heaven or hell."

—Buddha

LIGHTHOUSE

"Our deepest fear is not that we are inadequate. Our deepest fear is that we are powerful beyond measure. It is our light, not our darkness that most frightens us. We ask ourselves, 'Who am I to be brilliant, gorgeous, talented, fabulous?' Actually, who are you not to be? You are a child of God. Your playing small does not serve the world. There is nothing enlightened about shrinking so that other people won't feel insecure around you. We are all meant to shine, as children do. We were born to make manifest the glory of God that is within us. It's not just in some of us; it's in everyone. And as we let our own light shine, we unconsciously give other people permission to do the same. As we are liberated from our own fear, our presence automatically liberates others."

—Marianne Williamson, *Return to Love*

Recently I celebrated a friend's birthday. As the evening wore on, I grew tired and unfocused. A friend arrived late to the party. He seemed very focused and excited. Apparently his business deal went well. His light shone brightly. And I felt happy for him, not at all tired as I had been.

It had me thinking about how often we don't share our "wins" with each other for fear that we will make others jealous or feel bad about their lot. Wow. Not only do we dim our own light, we can't see the light in others when we withhold. Sure, we risk the possible petty comments from others who might be dimming their light and hoping that they won't be "called out." Yet, in holding ourselves back, we don't give those who are ready to risk the option of seeing a pathway before them.

My daughter received a new car. She's a responsible driver with more than average responsibility in her life. These rewards keep coming to her with things like a new job, a part in a community theater play and one in an adult theater play, more accolades at school as she's inducted into the Beta Club. The friends that she has who are supportive and happy for her "wins" will likely do well themselves. And those who are not, who find themselves lamenting all that they do *not* have, will create more lack in their lives.

Again, jealousy is a map to what you want. Notice where you encourage the light in others. Notice how the warmth of that encouragement lights *your* fire. When you shine brightly for yourself and others, it will also show you where the shadows fall.

Keep shining and move toward the light!

"The bamboo which bends is stronger than the oak which resists."

—Japanese proverb

HEROES

As a coach I'm always looking at my clients as though they are in their power, their magnificence, their joy and enthusiasm for life. One of my favorite things to do is to ask a client, "Who is your favorite superhero?" It tells me what qualities they value. And then if it's not clear to me, I asked them to describe their superhero to me. If they don't have one, I ask them to make one up. I will be writing more about superheroes in the coming year because I think the world needs more of us to step up. In the meantime, I ask *you*, dear reader, who is *your* superhero? Who is it that you remind yourself of when you are fully empowered?

Personal power is where we go when we're looking to see if we are being a victim of our circumstances, victim to another person, victim to an idea, or victim to a belief? We can even be victim to our own tiredness. So one of the questions I often ask clients then is, "What if you *could* do or accomplish that—what would happen if you did?" Coaches know how to make those distinctions between victim and responsible.

The general public appears to be looking for accountability everywhere these days. And many are willing to go with the shame/blame game. Chances are if your client is going to the shame/blame game, you likely are, too. So when you see that show up, step back and ask yourself, "What if I was just interested in results? What is my intention here?"

That mirror of course tells you everything.

Asking someone to define their superhero is usually a question I follow with, "What is your favorite song? What is the song you play when nobody's watching you? What song makes you want to dance around the house?" It usually surprises me what people choose. I call those "touchstones." It's what people conjure up when people are in their funk.

If your client comes to the phone and is off of his or her game, it helps to ask, "Who are you being when you wear your superhero?" The next question, "Will you bring that to mind and embody it?" And then, "How would you approach this situation?"

It is amazing what people can accomplish by simply owning their power.

"Frozen in fear, you avoid responsibility because you think your experience is beyond your control. This stance keeps you from making decisions, solving problems, or going after what you want in life."

—David Emerald

Boot Camp

A few weeks ago I went to what I'll call Boot Camp in South Carolina. It was wonderful. I was in an environment that encouraged exercise, eating well, getting rest, socializing ,and , I had a coach on site.

I exercised three or four times a day. I enjoyed wonderfully prepared meals. And I stayed in a condo with a couple of other people, people I did not know. One of these folks had gone to see the life coach. She had some things that she was trying to choose in her life. It was interesting how much she loved her session.

I went to this coaches' lecture and I found it to be really loving, caring, and well prepared. I felt she was a very effective coach for a lot of people, and particularly for those who needed that sort of supporting, loving nature.

I thought how different my coaching practice is from that of a life coach. I do coach the whole life, yet, I find that I attract executive level, powerful people. People who generally need vulnerability, and, at the same time, very tough love.

This coach came up to me and said something about giving away her power. She also told me that many coaches came to that Boot Camp. She felt that many of the coaches just needed to not be responsible for a while. Wow. It was nice to be offered a shoulder to lean on, however I realized that I could have been encouraged to be dependent on this coach.

I thought, "What a mirror for me!" Here I was being a victim to my tired legs, being a victim to not sleeping well because I was sore. And here she was talking about giving your power away. Fortunately, I was clued into what she was saying. We coaches have a way of listening to each other and sometimes seeing how we measure up. I was open to what she had to say. And I noticed that I was mirroring for myself a victim conversation.

It is my fervent belief that you *cannot* give your power away. If I could, I would never have trouble with my iPhone losing any juice. I believe you either own your power or you don't, that if we can give our power away it always leads to a victim stance.

But that made a big difference for me—having that encounter with someone who is talking at a high-level. It made such a difference for me that I got on the basketball court the next day and put in a fair show. I was very proud and yes, I played the comparison game. I realized that I was playing opposite someone who is three times younger than me. I felt very proud of that.

Owning your power can look many different ways.

"What lies in our power to do, it lies in our power not to do."

—Aristotle

TREAD SOFTLY

We have an epidemic in the world. People tend to equate personal power with "power over" someone else. This simply isn't true. Owning your power tends to help everyone!

And when owning our power, it really appears that we aren't "exercising" power, either. Personal power treads softly.

"Within you right now is the power to do things you never dreamed possible. This power becomes available to you just as soon as you can change your beliefs."

—Maxwell Malt

NEVER COMPLAIN, NEVER EXPLAIN

Never complain, never explain. Complaining or explaining means we are blaming someone. So.what do we do about this? Never complain. Diane Sawyer said in her interview with Oprah—I don't know if it was her father who said this to her or if it was her philosophy of life—that a complaint is really a poor question or a poor request. So when you're complaining, there is something that you want to be different.

A *positive* moving forward of that—again, we're not trying to look back into our history, we're looking forward to keep moving forward in our lives—would be to make a positive request. For example, "Oh man, it's so hot in here! Why can't they ever regulate the temperature?" When someone is explaining something to you over and over again, they are feeling like they are not good enough or not deserving or whatever, so listen for that. And if it's you doing that you might say to yourself, "Okay, how might I be accountable for my actions? How might I do something different if I was given the same choices?" You want to keep redefining things.

So if you find yourself defending yourself a lot, make a choice about what you're going to do different in your life.

Never complain. Never explain.

CONCLUSION

The Seven Keys are here for you, unearthed and available to you. I can show and describe them but only you can pick them up and approach your goals and dreams with them, ready to unlock the barriers so many others find impassable. It's my hope that you *try* them after understanding them, that you perfect their use, that you use this and all books on the subject to improve first your own life and then the lives of your clients. I hope they become second nature to you. All of us can benefit massively from a knowledge of the Seven Keys and if we coach others they become even more important, so that we and our clients can create what we want, right where we are. We no longer need to wonder, be frustrated, or seek the approval of others or even the environment.

Armed with this book series you can make a difference. These books are not the fastest route, however, to learning the Seven Keys and their application. That comes from a live event, where through your own commitment and focus, your results will be fast and powerful. See the back of this book to discover how you can attend a seminar or webinar, how you can become certified in the training of others in The Seven Keys, and how you too can benefit from receiving coaching as well as from delivering it. It might be easier than you think to get connected, but even were it not, what would it be worth to train in tapping into your own massive creativity? What about your clients?

And never think that seeking improvement suggests you lack in any way. You have all you need right now, right where you are. The trick is getting to it. We are each whole and complete beings, with untapped potential and an opportunity for actualization. We can each make our dreams come true. Holding a client, friend, or loved one to a higher standard is also not to make less of someone, but more, especially if they themselves desire it. Many don't seem to desire it simply because they are unaware or do not believe it's possible. We know better.

You are uniquely you, and the only one. And you are complete. You only need to unlock what lies inside.

I hope that you take these keys and unlocking your barriers, live the life I believe you deserve. I hope you find abundance in all you seek in whatever arenas you find you love, and in whatever form this may be. I hope you find this all to be an incredible adventure, because it is just that—the adventure of *you*. And you have gifts for the world, that the world needs and needs badly.

Give a man a fish and he eats for perhaps a day, but teach him to fish and he can feed himself, his family, his friends and community as long as there are fish. And when we create abundance for those around us we seem to have it ourselves. When we see strength, intelligence, goodness in others and grant them as much we have effectively created those things or at least planted the seeds of those things. The opposite is, well, the opposite. *Pity*, for example. When given or received leads to weakness and a weakened relationship as well. Any immediate gratification is short lived, of course. In fact taken to an extreme, this is the road to resentment! Giving when you lack leads only to more lack if you are giving only with the intention of feeling better or bigger yourself. Giving from a place of abundance however, creates it for everyone.

Giving with the idea of improving someone else's life *while also* improving your own is about one of life's greatest answers. The greatest partnerships—whether it's a husband and wife, business partners, or even a coach and client—are created by two wholly independent people who choose to be together because they can and want to be together. Partnerships created out of dependency leave one partner stronger than the other. They spiral downward as they are based on contraction, lack, and fear.

Yet we are, each of us, whole and complete beings.

And there is nothing broken about you or your clients, only untapped, locked away, in ways unique to each client. In fact we only do maintenance and development here, the repair shop is somewhere else. And part of that development is first recognizing, which is easy to do, the magnificence in each person. All you need to do is look.

May you celebrate your magnificence and that of each client through a life of passionate work and sound knowledge, may you and those you help then bring your own special gifts to the world!

Grounded in the Key of Oneness,

Understanding the influence of the Key of Inter-
Dimension,

Executing the Key of Movement,

Choosing in the Key of Paradox,

Sharing in the Key of Exchange,

Owning the Key of Personal Power,

You create what you most want the most, in yourself and
in others!

"There are many different kinds of power. True power comes from serving and helping others. Such behavior makes people respect you. They are willing to listen to your views and advice, and they support you. The energy of many people is thus channeled through one person. This kind of power is positive and authentic."

—Dalai Lama

THE 7 KEYS

TO CREATING THE LIFE YOU HAVE DREAMED OF!

Key #1, Oneness

Key #2, Inter-Dimension

Key #3, Movement

Key #4, Paradox

Key #5, Exchange

Key #6, Personal Power

Key #7, Yin~Yang

COMPANION JOURNAL

"Immense power is acquired by assuring yourself in your secret reveries that you were born to control affairs."

—Andrew Carnegie

Exercise ~ Be Your Superhero

1. Who is your superhero?

2. Write down ten characteristics of a superhero as you define them. (Sometimes we can define them by what they are not, if it makes it easier.)

3. Stand as though you are in your superhero power; plant your feet like Superman, or Xena, or Wonder Woman. (There *is* a superhero stance.)

4. Stand in that superhero posture for two minutes.

5. Breathe deeply.

6. Imagine that you are embodying that superhero.

7. Now, imagine that you're talking to your clients.

8. How does this alter your approach.?

9. What would it be like if you stood in your superhero posture before your coaching calls every day?

Exercise ~ What Stopped You?

1. Think of a time when you wanted to say something to someone and did not.

2. Experience the sensation in your body, and listen to the voice in your head.

3. Where is the sensation; what is the voice saying?

4. Now think of a time you wanted to do something and didn't.

5. What stopped you?

6. How might you make a different choice next time?

7. Now remember a time when you just knew that nothing could stop you, a time that all cylinders were firing.

8. Experience the sensation in your body and listen to the voice in your head.

9. Where is the sensation; what is the voice saying?

10. Now think of something that you know you will need to take action on in the near future.

11. How might the Key of Personal Power assist you?

Exercise ~ Unlocking with The Keys

The key of oneness explains the idea that if we are arguing with someone in this part of the world, this leaves a mark on someone else in another place. It's not a chain reaction or anything as clearly direct, yet it has an effect just the same. It explains why Mother Teresa would say, "You will not see me at an anti-war rally. If you have a peace rally, please invite me." She understood oneness, as well as polarity or paradox and expansion versus contraction. She knew we are all connected, she knew to focus on the thing that is the highest and best good to get the results she wanted, and she also knew that what she placed her attention on would expand.

All of the keys overlap. The process of creativity is integrated and happens regardless of what we think about it. We are always breathing, our blood is always pumping. We create new cells in our body every second. With every thought that we think; we are creating. At the level of thought and emotion, we can affect things in the world that we do not see.

In the following exercise, when we tested it, we found that it was effective in demonstrating that we can affect others simply by our thoughts and feelings. I was surprised when we discovered that the person with their eyes closed would often respond or react and not even be aware of their reactions! I see this exercise now as a way to illustrate the key of exchange, the key of oneness, the key of inter-dimension, the key of paradox, the key of personal power on a subtle level. However, I believe it applies best to the key of movement as it clearly shows we affect others by our own thoughts, and that once we accept that we do, we can affect everything around us by never even saying a word.

1. Put one person in the front of the room with their eyes closed or blindfolded.

2. You or someone else act as facilitator, and you whisper to other participants a word such as joy, sexiness, frustration, etc.

3. The participants go up one by one and without saying a word, they do their best to generate the word that they are given in the person who has their eyes closed.

4. After a short while ask the person at the front of the room to open his or her eyes or remove the blindfold, and talk about their thoughts during the exercise.

"A good indignation brings out all one's powers."

—Ralph Waldo Emerson

ABOUT BETSY JORDAN

Betsy Jordan holds a PhD in Experiential Training through the Legacy Center, and Direct Impact. Further training in leadership development and coaching helped her focus on how we can effectively cause transformation in our lives and businesses. "The river that runs through my career is the exciting world of human development." She has studied with Deepak Chopra, MD., becoming one of the first mind/body educators in the country. "Studying with Deepak helped me to see the science behind thoughts causing reactions in our bodies". That degree opened doors for her work in quality customer service with major corporations in hospital supplies and banking industries. Betsy has a BS in Business Administration from the University of North Carolina at Chapel Hill.

Betsy's life experiences have encompasses the creative community, the corporate world and the unique challenges of entrepreneurship. Whatever challenges you face, she is the coach who can relate, resolve problems, and turbo-charge your results. Her pioneering work on creativity is published in her book, *Seven Absolute Keys to Create Anything!* as well as a number of forthcoming publications. Please watch for new titles and materials as they are released.

START TODAY!

THE TIME TO BEGIN your perfecting of the seven keys is *right now*. Your full life of passion, your independence from waiting on politicians to gain their senses or the film industry to seek you out is at hand.

www.BullsEyeCoach.com

SEMINARS & WEBINARS

FIND OUT ABOUT UPCOMING seminars and webinars by visiting this website:

www.BullsEyeCoach.com

COACHING

AND FOR YOUR QUICKEST route to perfecting the seven tactics and to experience The BullsEyeCoaching™ process (which includes the seven tactics), *contact me today.* I look forward to meeting you and hearing your ideas!

info@BullsEyeCoach.com

ACKNOWLEDGEMENTS

THIS IS A WORK about life. I could say that I thank everyone who ever touched my life directly and indirectly for all of you have been teachers, and I mean that sincerely. In this way, you all have contributed to the writing of this book.

To my mentors, all of you: Ray, Michael, Lori, Rob, James, Sam. Let me leave a special notice to my mentor, Deepak Chopra, whose groundbreaking work in the psycho-physiological origins of disease taught me so much about how the mind and the body are related. Through Carolyn Myss in her *Anatomy of the Spirit* I recognize that even in irreverence there is still reverence.

Thanks to Louise Hay whose bravery and generosity has helped so many people overcome ailments in the body. To my mentors at the legacy center, Robb and Lori in particular, I thank you so much for the true stand you are in the world for so many people. For my mentor Michael Strasner who sees the humor in all things and always finds that balance.

To my former husbands both of whom taught me the extraordinary strength and power of faith. To the great loves of my life who are numerous and so I would rather they know who they are and be grateful that we had that love. Once I choose to love someone, I *always* do, even if we disagree.

Sean Roach, I wouldn't have ever thought about writing these books if not for your brilliance and direction. And Rodney Miles, thank you so much for your contribution above expectations and execution of this series. I look forward to many, many years with this team of amazing people.

To the boys of my heart, Kyle and Taylor, who taught me that parenting had nothing to do with being of the same genetic make-up. And finally, to my sensitive and brilliant daughter who shows me every day what a miracle life is.

THE CHAKRAS

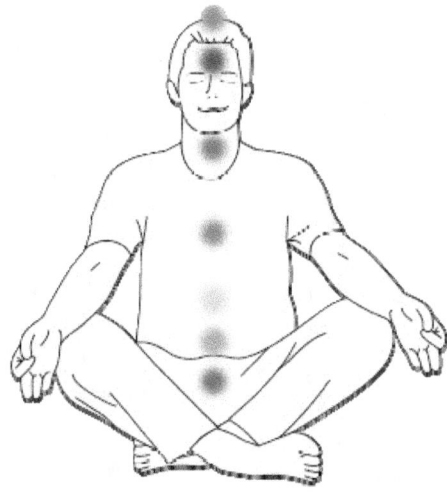

Figure 1: The seven chakras and their locations in the body.

The word "chakra" comes from a Sanskrit word meaning "wheel," (or "spinning point of light) and in some religions of India are considered points of energy and part of the intangible body that influences the physical body. Energy channels through these points. While there are believed to be many and various *nodes* or chakras throughout our bodies, these are the seven most important.

According to Caroline Myss in her book *Anatomy of the Spirit*, all of our thoughts and experiences are filtered through these chakras which function in part as databases, and are associated with our physical and mental selves as well as certain colors.

Some associate the chakras with specific nerve centers and glandular functions, and each is associated with various energies, all of which can be understood and placed into harmony.

THE 7 KEYS

TO CREATING THE LIFE YOU HAVE DREAMED OF!

Key #1, Oneness

Key #2, Inter-Dimension

Key #3, Movement

Key #4, Paradox

Key #5, Exchange

Key #6, Personal Power

Key #7, Yin~Yang

7 KEYS SUMMARIES

Key 1, Oneness

Oneness, all, we are the same stuff, we affect and are affected by each other, remove judgment of self and others.

Located above the head. 7th Chakra.

Key 2, Inter-Dimension

Inter-dimension, all levels, all of the time, awareness at the level of "before language," thoughts become things, know what you "know."

Located between the eyes (third eye). 6th Chakra.

Key 3, Movement

Movement, constant motion even at subtle levels... everything moving, language is the great creator, in the beginning was the Word, Thumper in the movie *Bambi* was correct: "If you can't say somethin' nice, don't say nothin' at all." Even subtler, if you can't "think "anything nice, then don't think anything at all, or at the very least, get outta the room!

Located at the throat (voice box). 5th Chakra.

Key 4, Paradox

Paradox, in every challenge lies the seed of its solution. Opposites exist. Polarity. Focus on positive and dismiss all lack and thoughts of lack. Want lots of goodies in your life, warm and fuzzies? Create it for others. Want love? Create it in every interaction. What we focus on expands. Decide with the heart.

Located above the heart. 4th Chakra.

Key 5, Exchange

Exchange, the Universe (God) rewards expansive plans. Giving and receiving both are expansive actions. Taking is a contracting energy—it interrupts expansion and leads to contraction. Give what you most want in a manner that creates this for others. Associated with gut feeling or solar plexus.

Located above the solar plexus. 3rd Chakra.

Key 6, Personal Power

Personal power, we are all whole and complete, no matter what our size and shape, number of fingers and toes, we can never give our power away. In our most complete and powerful understanding of ourselves, we understand the laws of cause and effect. We are able to respond to it all. Owning our power means that we have released "victim" consciousness. From the place of personal strength, ownership of it all, we can create something different. There is nothing more powerful than *you!*

Located above the abdomen. 2nd Chakra.

Key 7, Yin/Yang

Male/female, there lies within us the feminine and masculine principles and properties of creativity. Feminine is nurturing, gestational, conceptual, and spiritual. Masculine is assertive, action-oriented, physical, and material. When in balance, beautiful and powerful creations are born. When out of balance, depression and sometimes even war ensue.

Located at the root or genital area. 1st Chakra.

7 KEYS & THE CHAKRAS

Key #1, Oneness
Located above the head. 7th Chakra.

Key #2, Inter-Dimension
Located between the eyes (third eye). 6th Chakra.

Key #3, Movement
Located at the throat (voice box). 5th Chakra.

Key #4, Paradox
Located above the heart. 4th Chakra.

Key #5, Exchange
Located above the solar plexus. 3rd Chakra.

Key #6, Personal Power
Located above the abdomen. 2nd Chakra.

Key #7, Yin~Yang
Located at the root or genital area. 1st Chakra.

SUCCESS STORIES

The following case studies assure you that the process works! And this format keeps us from sharing confidential information.

THE LESSON

Do it Your Way

A frustrated employee turned budding entrepreneur discovered her true path.

This client came to me knowing that things weren't right at work. She'd known this for awhile. She wanted guidance. In pattern interruption the image she pulled was of her on the beach talking with Jesus. (This image is always the perfect one for you, chosen by you, in the perfect time to answer your intended result.) His words, according to what she saw were, "You go back and do what you need to do. I am with you. I've done this my way, you do it your way." I watched her progress from afar. After this experience, she had the courage to start her business. It is gradually growing—her way. It's a great gift to the world, and a great gift from her heart. The image she held in her mind's eye that day gave her strength, courage and insight to boldly proceed in the direction of her dreams.

THE LESSON

The Power of Saying, "No"

A very powerful educated attorney had a vision, yet didn't know what to do about it.

My trademarked seven-step TurboCoaching program showed us that the step involving personal power was out of balance. Once this client got clear on his vision for his company, he was able to make requests with urgency. This got him an audience with a major U.S. corporate CEO which led to a future relationship with that corporate leader. Two months was all he needed. His life and his work were transformed, and his vision came to life.

THE LESSON
Don't Ignore the Shadow Side

Yet another study involved a public relations professional.

Her life was grounded in involvement with people. She knew her professional life was in good shape; yet her personal relationships would falter. She chose pattern interruption and discovered a subconscious stumbling block. The image in her subconscious was of her dad. During the session she pulled an image showing that she adored him, and then, she saw a dark side that she had never consciously acknowledged. Through the interpretation session she was able to see that she denied the shadow side in any of her relationships. Once she was aware of this pattern of denial, she was able to create relationships with people which were authentic, embracing both the lighter and darker sides of their personalities. When those sides were extreme, she could walk away without harm.